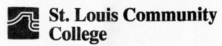

GREAT MYSTERIES

Pyramids

OPPOSING VIEWPOINTS®

Look for these and other exciting *Great Mysteries:
Opposing Viewpoints* books:

GREAT MYSTERIES

Pyramids

OPPOSING VIEWPOINTS®

by Michael O'Neal

Greenhaven Press, Inc.   P.O. Box 289009, San Diego, California 92198-9009

Library of Congress Cataloging-in-Publication Data

O'Neal, Michael, 1949-.
    Pyramids : opposing viewpoints / by Michael J. O'Neal.
        p.   cm. — (Great mysteries)
    Includes bibliographical references and index.
    ISBN 1-56510-216-9   (alk. paper)
    1. Pyramids—Egypt—Juvenile literature.   [1. Pyramids—
Egypt.   2. Egypt—Antiquities.]   I. O'Neal, Michael, 1949-
Pyramids.   II. Title.   III. Series: Great mysteries (Saint Paul, Minn.)
DT63.054   1995
726'.8'0932—dc20   94-22468
                                                                CIP
                                                                AC

*This one's for Mom,
whose influence will prove as enduring
as anything the ancient Egyptians
built.*

Contents

Introduction

This book is written for the curious—those who want to explore the mysteries that are everywhere. To be human is to be constantly surrounded by wonderment. How do birds fly? Are ghosts real? Can animals and people communicate? Was King Arthur a real person or a myth? Why did Amelia Earhart disappear? Did history really happen the way we think it did? Where did the world come from? Where is it going?

Great Mysteries: Opposing Viewpoints books are intended to offer the reader an opportunity to explore some of the many mysteries that both trouble and intrigue us. For the span of each book, we want the reader to feel that he or she is a scientist investigating the extinction of the dinosaurs, an archaeologist searching for clues to the origin of the great Egyptian pyramids, a psychic detective testing the existence of ESP.

One thing all mysteries have in common is that there is no ready answer. Often there are *many* answers but none on which even the majority of authorities agrees. *Great Mysteries: Opposing Viewpoints* books introduce the intriguing views of the experts, allowing the reader to participate in their explorations, their theories, and their disagreements as they try to explain the mysteries of our world.

But most readers won't want to stop here. These *Great Mysteries: Opposing Viewpoints* aim to stimulate the reader's curiosity. Although truth is often impossible to discover, the search is fascinating. It is up to the reader to examine the evidence, to decide whether the answer is there—or to explore further.

"Penetrating so many secrets, we cease to believe in the unknowable. But there it sits nevertheless, calmly licking its chops."

H.L. Mencken, American essayist

Prologue

Enigmas in Stone

The men had tunneled through the stone of the immense and mysterious ancient pyramid for nearly a hundred frustrating feet. They were looking for the secret passageway that would take them to the end of their quest for hidden treasure. Progress had been slow. The stone was hard, the desert sun merciless, and with each foot, the tunnel had become darker, dustier, and hotter.

At the point of giving up, one man suddenly heard something, a soft, muffled sound, as if an object inside the stone structure had fallen. The man was excited. The sound suggested that they were near a passageway or secret chamber.

The men renewed their efforts, altering their tunnel direction toward the sound. After burrowing for only a few more feet, they burst through the rock to a narrow passageway. With mounting excitement they followed the passageway as it angled down, but found only an empty pit at the bottom. Retracing their steps, they found midway up the passage a second passage that seemed to angle upward from the first. This passage, however, was blocked by a massive granite plug. On the floor near the plug was a carved, jeweled stone, whose fall may have caused the sound the workman heard. The

(Opposite page) A bird's eye view of one of the Giza pyramids. Even today, these huge stone monuments remain shrouded in mystery, tantalizing thousands of visitors each year.

stone's beauty and rarity hinted that this tunnel held the object of their quest.

Their excitement renewed, the men bored around the plug, only to find another, then another. Behind the three granite plugs was a series of softer limestone plugs, which they were able to break apart and clear away piece by piece. For days the men worked, until finally they forced their way into the ascending passage. Crawling on their hands and knees, they came to a small, empty chamber at the end of a short, horizontal detour. They returned to the ascending passageway, which suddenly opened into a magnificent narrow gallery. It was five or six times a man's height and a hundred feet or more long. Continuing upward, the men finally arrived at a large chamber. It contained only an empty sarcophagus, that is, a large stone coffin. It was made of dark, polished granite. The men searched the room frantically, seeking the jewels and treasure they had hoped to find. In the fury of their disappointment they ripped up the floor and tore at the walls. One legend tells that the leader of the party, to appease his men, hid a stash of gold in the chamber and allowed them to find it later. In any event, the disappointed explorers abandoned the structure, sealing the entrance they had made. The scene of their labors rested undisturbed in the Egyptian desert for the next four centuries.

Al Mamun's Disappointment

The leader of the expedition, Abdullah Al Mamun, was no looter or tomb robber. He was an Arab caliph—a ruler who was thought to be a successor to Muhammad, the seventh-century prophet and founder of Islam. In the ninth century Al Mamun turned the Persian city of Baghdad into a center of learning, complete with its own library and astronomical observatory. He ransacked the area around the Mediterranean Sea in search of manuscripts about mathematics, astronomy, navigation, philoso-

phy—anything that would bring enlightenment to the Arab world. He was familiar with the legends that the massive pyramid on the Giza Plateau in Egypt had magical powers and contained treasure. These legends, after all, were recounted in *A Thousand and One Nights*, the series of stories told by Queen Scheherazade to stave off her execution at the hands of her jealous husband. But when Al Mamun learned the Great Pyramid had a secret chamber that contained maps, mathematical tables, and globes that would unlock the secrets of the earth, he was determined to find out for himself. The men he

Seeking jewels and other treasure, Al Mamun expresses disappointment in the near empty structure of the Great Pyramid. Al Mamun's expedition in A.D. 820 was the first known exploration of the Great Pyramid.

hired to help him penetrate the pyramid were disappointed that they did not find a trove of gold and jewels. But their disappointment must have paled next to that of Al Mamun, who failed to find the great knowledge he was seeking.

Al Mamun's expedition in A.D. 820 was the first known exploration of the Great Pyramid at Giza, one of dozens of pyramids that form a sort of artificial mountain range along the west bank of Egypt's Nile River. Although a handful of explorers made weak efforts to enter the pyramid in the years after Al Mamun's attempt, most were frightened off by the superstitions and legends of curses that surrounded it. Not until the seventeenth century did serious interest in the pyramids revive as European

Generations of researchers have probed the pyramids and their surrounding areas, posing conflicting theories about how and why the pyramids were built.

travelers became intrigued by the mystery of the great monuments' origins.

In the nineteenth and twentieth centuries swarms of archaeologists and historians have explored the pyramids, measuring them, probing their interiors, and speculating on how and why they were built. They have found some answers and offered many conflicting and intriguing theories. And they have come away from the pyramids as awed and mystified as Al Mamun must have been over a thousand years ago. For nearly five thousand years the pyramids have stood—mute, immune to earthquake, flood, and time. These enigmas, these mysteries in stone, still hoard their secrets for new generations of explorers, tantalizing them with unanswered, perhaps unanswerable, questions.

One

A Triumph of the Ancient World

A person standing atop virtually any building in Cairo, Egypt, and scanning the western horizon takes in an arresting sight: that of the Great Pyramid at Giza floating hauntingly above the eastern edge of the Sahara Desert. Nearby, like minor luminaries paying homage to a larger, brighter star, are five other pyramids, two fairly large, three tiny by comparison. The ancient Greeks regarded the pyramids on the Giza Plateau as the greatest of the Seven Wonders of the World. Perhaps they were right, for the pyramids, the earliest known buildings made entirely of stone, are the only one of the ancient Seven Wonders to have survived to today.

Etched against the desert sky, the pyramids at Giza, with the Sphinx nearby, are the most familiar of the pyramids, but they are not the only ones. Some eighty or more pyramids range up and down the west bank of the Nile River, roughly between Cairo on the north and Aswan to the south, though most are within fifty miles of Cairo. Some of these pyramids were never completed; many had to be dug out of the shifting sands of the desert by later explorers; and still others may lie undiscovered under those sands, waiting for a persistent seeker to bring them to light. The Egyptians left behind no

(Opposite page) Like a silent guard, the Sphinx looms before the pyramids of Giza, the most familiar of the pyramids.

written records describing how and why the pyramids were built. Some historians, such as Basil Stewart, author of *The Mystery of the Great Pyramid*, believe invaders from other lands built them. Other historians and archaeologists have different theories. Perhaps somewhere in the fertile Nile Valley—in a tomb, an ancient temple, an undiscovered chamber in one of the pyramids—such a record waits, ready to answer questions that have had no answers for thousands of years.

The Nile Valley

Most of Egypt consists of desert. To the east is the Arabian Desert, which ends at the rim of the

Since prehistoric times, Egyptians have made their homes along the banks of the Nile River, which cuts through the vast North African desert.

Gulf of Suez and the Red Sea. To the west is the relentless Sahara. Cleaving the two deserts is Egypt's lifeline, the Nile River, which flows northward from its source in Africa into the Mediterranean Sea. The Egyptians have clustered along an approximately seven-hundred-mile stretch of this river since prehistoric times.

For much of its early history Egypt was populated by small warring tribes. These tribes lived in small territories, or provinces, called nomes. No central government existed. The tribes in Upper and Lower Egypt gave their allegiance to two competing rulers. (Lower Egypt was downriver, closer to the Mediterranean; Upper Egypt was upriver, to the south.) Around 3200 B.C., however, Egypt united under one pharaoh, beginning a long series of what the ancient Greek historians called dynasties, or families of kings. The dynasties ruled Egypt for roughly three thousand years.

Following the practice of the Greeks, modern historians group these dynasties into the Old, Middle, and New Kingdoms, each separated from the preceding one by an important historical event. Most of the pyramids were built during the Old Kingdom, in the Third through the Sixth Dynasties—that is, from about 2685 to 2180 B.C. The largest and most elaborate of the pyramids were built during the Third and Fourth Dynasties, in a 160-year span from 2650 to 2490 B.C.

Scattered Villages

During the First and Second Dynasties, Egypt was still less a nation than a collection of scattered villages. The people lived along the banks of the Nile, farming, tending cattle, and occasionally passing the time by going to war with one another. Each year the Nile flooded for three months, irrigating the land and leaving behind fresh silt deposits that kept the land fertile and productive. Many historians think the later pharaohs took advantage of these floods to

Egyptian laborers as they might have appeared thousands of years ago.

recruit the thousands of laborers—made idle by the floods—needed to construct the pyramids.

Peace came to the Nile Valley during the Third Dynasty. Historians know little about the pharaohs who imposed this peace. They do know, however, that the first pyramid was built at Saqqara some time after 2700 B.C. This pyramid, built for the pharaoh Djoser, or Zoser, was called the Step Pyramid because its six tiers, each smaller than the one below, give the pyramid the appearance of a staircase. Historians also know something about the pyramid's builder, whose name was Imhotep. To later dynasties, Imhotep was a legendary, almost godlike figure. He was a physician, a scientist, Djoser's chief advisor, and the founder of a school of architecture that provided the designers and builders of the lavish pyramids built in the Fourth Dynasty. Thanks largely to Imhotep's vision Egyptian architecture progressed rapidly from the crude thatched and mud-brick huts that housed peasants to imposing palaces and temples made of wood and stone to the far more imposing pyramids, designed to last forever. "All things dread Time," says an ancient Arab proverb, "but Time dreads the Pyramids."

The Step Pyramid at Saqqara was the first pyramid, but it was by no means the last. Another fa-

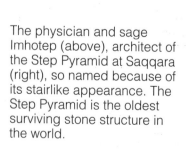

The physician and sage Imhotep (above), architect of the Step Pyramid at Saqqara (right), so named because of its stairlike appearance. The Step Pyramid is the oldest surviving stone structure in the world.

mous pyramid is at Dahshûr, built around 2600 B.C. for King Sneferu. It is called the Bent Pyramid: the pyramid seems to bulge outward because of a slight bend in each of its sides about midway up. Another major pyramid, also attributed to Sneferu, is the one at Medûm. It is just under three hundred feet tall, but it sits on a hill, making it a breathtaking landmark for miles around.

The high point of the pyramid era came at Giza. There, over a twenty-three-year period, King Khufu built the most famous of the pyramids, the Great Pyramid, during the twenty-fifth century B.C. (In books about ancient Egypt, Khufu is often referred to as Cheops, the name the Greek historians gave

The pyramids of Giza cut a striking silhouette against the desert sky.

King Khafre succeeded Khufu. Khafre built his steeply angled pyramid near Khufu's Great Pyramid.

him.) Little is known about Khufu. Some legends say he was a hated tyrant. But he was responsible for a great deal of construction throughout Egypt, and during the following centuries his name became a kind of magical charm.

Khufu's successor, Khafre (Khephren to the Greeks), built his pyramid nearby. Although somewhat smaller than the Great Pyramid, it gives the appearance of being the same size because it sits on slightly higher ground and because its sides are at a steeper angle. Khafre is the subject of perhaps one of the most famous Egyptian statues, a stone bust of him with a hawk perched on his shoulder, found in the temple attached to the pyramid.

The comparatively humble pyramid of King Menkaure (Mycerinus to the Greeks) is the last of the three large pyramids. Evidence shows that the so-called Third Pyramid was restored many centuries later in the Twenty-sixth Dynasty. Menkaure had the three smallest Giza pyramids built for his queens.

The Great Pyramid at Giza

All the pyramids hold interest for archaeologists, for each adds something to their understanding of the art, architecture, and social customs of the ancient Egyptians. Because of its size, however, the Great Pyramid at Giza has held the most fascination for generations of scholars and tourists. For centuries visitors have stood at the base of the Great Pyramid and wondered: Why would a pharaoh devote so much time and so many resources to a structure that has so little apparent use? How could laborers working without wheels, horses, or pulleys, and equipped with tools made largely of copper (a soft metal), have constructed something so large, so precise, and so enduring?

The Great Pyramid lies about ten miles west of Cairo on a one-mile-square plateau that rises more than a hundred feet above the Nile Valley. The Pyramid itself covers an area of thirteen acres, made perfectly level to within a fraction of an inch. The Pyramid is made of more than two and a half million stone blocks, each one weighing between two and seventy tons, although the average weight is about two and a half tons. If the Pyramid was built over a twenty-three-year period, then over 100,000 blocks per year, or about 275 per day, had to be cut, shaped, smoothed, transported, and raised to their positions in one of the 201 stepped levels, or courses, that reach 485 feet—the height of a modern forty-story building. Originally the Pyramid had an outer limestone casing, a covering of angled stones that fit into the corners formed by each step created by the square building stones. These casing stones gave the Pyramid a smooth, polished appearance.

Made up of over two and a half million stone blocks, the Great Pyramid's incredible size and precision continue to intrigue scientists.

"Between 2630 and 1640 B.C., Egyptian kings built for themselves tombs in the form of pyramids."

John Baines and Jaromír Málek, *Atlas of Ancient Egypt*

"I dated these constructions [the Giza pyramids] to circa 9000 B.C."

Zecharia Sitchin, *Fate*, July 1993

During the fourteenth century, however, people stripped off most of the casing stones and used them for construction projects in Cairo. Many of the buildings that stand in Cairo today are made from stones taken from the Great Pyramid.

A Labyrinth

Although the Great Pyramid is essentially solid, it contains a number of passageways and chambers, as Al Mamun discovered more than a thousand years ago. Partway up the northern slope is a sealed entrance to the descending passage, which angles down to an empty pit—perhaps originally intended for a burial chamber—about six hundred feet directly beneath the Pyramid's apex, or highest point. An ascending passage angles off from the descending passage. This passage leads first to a short horizontal passage, which in turn leads to what archaeologists call the Queen's Chamber because of its peaked ceiling, a feature normally found in queens' tombs of that era. The ascending passage continues, becoming the lofty Grand Gallery. This gallery—28 feet high and 157 feet long—leads directly to the King's Chamber, the site of an empty sarcophagus and of Al Mamun's disappointment. Additionally, four narrow air shafts, two from the Queen's Chamber and two from the King's Chamber, angle up to the outside of the Pyramid. It is possible that other passageways and chambers remain inside, waiting to be discovered.

The Great Pyramid does not stand alone. In common with most pyramids, it is surrounded by a complex of other structures. Many of these are mastabas, or small, pyramid-like tombs, in which numerous officials and members of the royal family are entombed. In most pyramids a long causeway leads from a point close to the river to a temple on the pyramid's east side; the Great Pyramid has such a causeway but, unlike the other pyramids at Giza, nothing remains of its temple. Most of these smaller structures, in fact, have either been covered by desert sand or partially dismantled by tourists, explorers, or builders.

Archaeologists and construction engineers continue to be amazed at the incredible precision with which the Great Pyramid was built, without any of the tools or machines that are taken for granted today. Its precision prompted Sir Flinders Petrie, British archaeologist and author of several books about the pyramids, to remark that the Pyramid "is to be compared to the finest opticians' work on a

The entrance to the Great Pyramid. Note the dwarfed appearance of the people mingling on the stone blocks that make up the Pyramid's lofty sides.

An elaborately decorated Egyptian mummy case. Today, most archaeologists and Egyptologists believe that the pyramids were built as massive resting places for such mummies.

scale of acres." The four sides of the Pyramid, for instance, face squarely north, south, east, and west, as accurately as if modern surveying implements had been used. Similarly, the lengths of the four sides differ by only .0088 percent, or eighty-eight thousandths of 1 percent. The ascending and descending passages have a uniform slope of twenty-six degrees.

One of the chief technical challenges the builders faced was getting the four sides to meet at a single imaginary point hundreds of feet above the base. If the slope of one of the sides had been off even a little, the side would have over- or undershot the others. Correcting the angle would have produced an unsightly bulge, as the builders of the Bent Pyramid learned. But no such bulge mars the perfect symmetry of the Great Pyramid.

Mysteries Abound

Many questions surround the Great Pyramid—all the pyramids, in fact. But they resolve into two fundamental ones: why and how? Why were the pyramids built? And how were they built?

Most archaeologists and Egyptologists—those who study ancient Egypt—believe that the pyramids were built as elaborate tombs for the pharaohs. Other researchers, however, offer competing theories: that the pyramids were public works projects designed to unify the nation, that they encoded biblical information, that they preserved for future generations mathematical formulas such as the one for *pi,* that they were built as astronomical observatories, surveyors' tools, calendars, or geographical landmarks. It is possible, of course, that the pyramids were intended to serve some combination of these and other purposes.

As for how the pyramids were built, archaeologists for many years were mystified, and they still disagree about details. But most now agree that the huge stone blocks were raised to their positions by teams of men who used ropes to pull the stones up a system of ramps built around the pyramid.

A final question that the pyramids raise is whether they are cursed in some way. It is true that a number of people associated with the pyramids have died or suffered accidents after exploring them, but their deaths have possible alternative explanations. Many people, too, believe that the pyramids have a mysterious power not only to kill but also to heal.

While many disdain the ideas of mysterious powers, those who have seen the pyramids firsthand agree on one thing: These magnificent structures do have power—the power to mystify, to inspire awe, and to challenge people to solve the many enigmas of the pyramids.

Two

Why Were the Pyramids Built?

(Opposite page) A late
nineteenth-century team of
archaeologists delve into
antiquity as they probe an
Egyptian pyramid site. Both
amateur and professional
archaeologists were common
sights in nineteenth-century
Egypt.

An Arab living in the vicinity of nineteenth-century Cairo was often greeted by the sight of foreign visitors on the docks, surrounded by trunks, and often accompanied by a spouse, even children. More often than not the travelers bargained in English for help with the trunks, though a smattering of French or Italian could sometimes be heard. The visitors' trunks were filled not only with provisions but also with tools and measuring devices. The visitors, determination in their eyes, had arrived to plumb the mysteries of the pyramids.

During the nineteenth century travel became easier, and many scientists and explorers were bent on learning about lands unknown to Europeans. As part of this interest in exotic and faraway places, waves of archaeologists, amateur and professional, invaded Egypt to poke and probe the pyramids. Each sailed home with a new theory to explain why the pyramids were built. The most widely accepted theory, then and today, is that when a new pharaoh ascended the throne, he ordered that a pyramid be built. The pyramid would serve as his tomb when he died. As far back as 1736 the British explorer John Greaves wrote in his book *Pyramidographia*: "That these Pyramids were intended for Sepulchres and

"These structures are royal tombs."

Dr. I. E.S. Edwards, curator of Egyptian antiquities at the British Museum

"While very few people will dispute that the pyramids had some connection with the afterlife of the pharaoh, the general statement that the pharaohs were buried in them is by no means indisputable."

Kurt Mendelssohn, *The Riddle of the Pyramids*

Monuments of the Dead, is the constant opinion of most authors which have writ of this argument." Greaves was confirming what the Greek historian Herodotus—the first pyramid historian—had written as far back as the fourth century B.C.

One factor that has led some authorities to question this theory is that, as tombs, the pyramids would have been incredibly costly. The nineteenth-century author Rudyard Kipling wrote, tongue in cheek:

> Who shall doubt the secret hid
> Under Cheops' pyramid
> Is that some contractor did
> Cheops out of several millions?

Death and the Afterlife

To understand why the pharaohs might have built such elaborate and expensive monuments to serve as their tombs, it is necessary to understand the importance the Egyptians attached to the after-

As depicted in this illustration, ancient Egyptians preserved dead bodies through mummification. To further protect the mummies, they may have housed them in the elusive chambers of the stone pyramids.

life. The ancient Egyptians firmly believed in life after death. Their belief was based on their complicated view of the nature of the individual and the soul, or spirit. They believed that in addition to the physical body, every person had a kind of replica, or double, called the *ka*. They also believed that the *ka* came into existence before the physical body did. The *ka* is different from what many people think of as the soul; the Egyptians called the soul the *ba*, or *bai*. Additionally, they believed in at least four other human principles, or parts, that survived the death of the physical body.

The *ka,* however, was the most important of the principles. The pharaohs believed that the *ka* did not have to die with the physical body. If, somehow, the body could be protected from decay, violence, and hunger, the *ka* would be immortal, and the pharaoh could assume his rightful place with the gods. Mummification satisfied one of these needs: by cleaning the body, removing its organs, soaking it in chemicals, wrapping it in long bandages, then interring, or burying, it in a human-shaped coffin, priests could preserve it from decay. The pyramid could satisfy the other two needs. It could protect the body from the ravages of violence and hunger. Its lofty height (the word *pyramid* comes from the Egyptian *pi-re-mus*, meaning "altitude") and its massive, stable form gave it permanence and strength against intruders. Also, the pyramid's chambers could be used to store food, water, and implements—anything the pharaoh would need in the other world. Artists could paint the walls with pictures of livestock, plows, or fields of grain. These representations, along with statues and busts, would serve the pharaoh in the afterlife just as well as the real things.

Tombs for the Pharaohs?

Considerable evidence supports the view that the pyramids were built chiefly as tombs for the pharaohs. Without exception, all the pyramids are

An Egyptian mummy on display at the Field Museum in Chicago. Thousands of years old, it attests to the effectiveness of the Egyptian mummification process.

ranged along the west bank of the Nile. This is significant because the west, the direction of the setting sun and the end of day, has always been closely associated in myth and literature with the journey to the afterlife. In ancient Egypt, the west bank of the Nile was thought of as the abode of the dead. Most pyramids also have a sloping entryway that points north, directly toward a cluster of stars that the ancient Egyptians identified with the realm of the gods. In effect, the entryway was also an exit through which the *ka* could pass in a direct line to the other world.

Additional support for the tomb theory comes from the pyramids' origins in the mastaba, a small, pyramid-like mausoleum used for burial purposes during the Old Kingdom. As time passed these mastabas became more elaborate and complex. The Step Pyramid at Saqqara represents a leap from the earlier mastabas to the true pyramids.

Empty Coffins

Indisputable, too, is the fact that most of the pyramids contain, or at one time did contain (according to historical accounts), a stone coffin. The coffin in the King's Chamber of the Great Pyramid was clearly put there while the Pyramid was being built. Archaeologists know this because the coffin is an inch bigger that the passageways leading to the chamber, making it impossible for the coffin to have been carried in later. The inclusion of the coffin supports the view that Khufu intended the Pyramid to be his burial place. Most of the coffins in the pyramids, like that in the King's Chamber, have been found empty, although a few have contained unidentified and undated remains. The usual explanation for the absence of bodies is that during nearly fifty centuries the coffins have been invaded and robbed by treasure seekers and the pharaohs' enemies. Whether any of the empty coffins ever contained bodies remains an unanswered question.

"The lack of evidence of burials bothers me; lately I've . . . wondered if they really were tombs of kings."

John Cooney, director, Brooklyn Museum's Egypt collection

"The fact that the sarcophagi in the Khufu and Khafre pyramids were found empty is easily explained as the work of the intruders."

Kurt Mendelssohn, *The Riddle of the Pyramids*

As its impression suggests, this oblong pit near Khufu's pyramid once housed a funeral boat.

The tomb theory is supported by at least one other piece of evidence. During the Old Kingdom it was customary for mourners to bear a funeral boat in the procession to the burial site. The boat was then buried alongside the tomb or mastaba, ready for the pharaoh to use to sail to the afterworld. Such boats have been found at Saqqara, Dahshûr, and, in 1954, at Giza. That year a large mound of dirt and debris was cleared away from the south side of the Great Pyramid to open a path for a new road. Underneath the mound workers found a long pit that had been closed with limestone blocks and sealed with plaster. When the ninety-three-foot-long pit was opened, a partially dismantled cedar-wood boat was found, nearly perfectly intact. Similar boats have been found around the queens' pyramids at Giza. The presence of these boats suggests that the pyramids were built as burial places for the pharaohs.

Nagging Questions

For most pyramid historians the case is closed. They believe that this evidence is proof that the tomb theory is correct. For others, however, a number of nagging questions remain. These questions do not necessarily disprove the tomb theory. But they have led some archaeologists and historians to offer alternative theories.

One question concerns the bareness of the walls in the Great Pyramid and other pyramids from the same time period. Egyptologist John Cooney told *National Geographic*, "It has always puzzled me that all pyramids from the time of Djoser in the Third Dynasty until near the end of the Fifth Dynasty are completely, utterly blank." This is in contrast to later tombs—the most famous of which is that of King Tutankhamen—which are marked by lavish, floor-to-ceiling paintings and other decorations. Many of these more ornate tombs were not even the tombs of pharaohs, leading scholars such as Cooney to wonder why Egypt's god-kings would receive less elaborate send-offs than lesser mortals.

In contrast to lavishly decorated tombs, some Egyptian tombs are devoid of paintings or other embellishments.

A detail of a tomb painting depicts ancient Egyptians treading grapes and storing wine in jars.

The inconsistencies do not stop there. Another concerns the King's Chamber and the unfinished pit beneath the Great Pyramid. In *The Great Pyramid in Fact and in Theory*, Egyptologist William Kingsland points out that in most pyramids, the passage leading to the burial chamber goes down into the bedrock beneath the pyramid, rather than up. Why Khufu would have left the pit of the Great Pyramid unfinished and had his coffin placed at the end of the *ascending* passage remains a mystery. Kingsland is also puzzled by the air shafts that run from the outside to the Queen's Chamber. Although they stop five inches short of the chamber, their presence suggests that the builders had some purpose in mind for the Queen's Chamber. Finally, Kingsland wonders why, if the Great Pyramid was built merely as a sealed tomb, so much attention was lavished on its construction—why, for example, the stonework had to be so meticulously accurate. For Kingsland the unwavering precision and accuracy of the Great Pyramid suggest that it might have been built for some other purpose.

Puzzling Questions

Some archaeologists, such as Dr. I.E.S. Edwards, a leading pyramid scholar and retired curator of Egyptian antiquities at the British Museum, are equally puzzled by the Grand Gallery. Archaeologists admire its flawless construction. Twenty- to thirty-ton blocks are so highly polished and positioned so accurately in the walls that their joints are only a hundredth of an inch thick. Edwards says that he has no idea what purpose the gallery served. But its strange and unexpected presence, blossoming near the end of the cramped and airless ascending passage, raises questions about whether the pyramids might have served some purpose other than as burial places.

Finally, Tom Melham, a writer for *National Geographic* magazine, wonders why the passageways are so narrow and cramped. He points out that it would have been extraordinarily difficult for crouching attendants to carry the pharaoh's remains up the steep passage. He wrote: "It's a vision that hardly holds with the dignified air of Egyptian funerary ritual." One response might be that the smaller passageways were easier to plug. This would make it harder for robbers to enter the burial chamber. As Melham points out, however, the Egyptians clearly did not lack the ability to plug up far larger passageways. And if Khufu *was* entombed in the King's Chamber and his body later stolen, why did the robbers go to the trouble of replugging the ascending passage?

One alternative to the tomb theory is that the pyramids were never intended to be actual tombs, but cenotaphs—that is, funeral memorials. In *Secrets of the Great Pyramid* Peter Tompkins raises the possibility that the sarcophagus in the King's

Chamber and the empty sarcophagi in other pyramids were intended as open tombs that symbolized the pharaoh's resurrection or that provided an earthly home for his *ka*. Corridors would not have to be very tall or wide for the spiritual double to pass through. In discussing this possibility, Melham wonders whether the pharaohs were buried in nearby cemeteries, where someday they might be discovered, or perhaps *under* the pyramids, where robbers could never reach them.

The Search for Alternative Theories

These questions have led pyramid scholars to search for alternative theories to explain why the pyramids were built. Instead of finding a workaday, practical purpose—burial—some scholars speculate that the pyramids have some sort of historical or cultural meaning. To some, the pyramids are a cipher—a puzzle or code—fashioned by their builders to pass information to future generations.

Physicist Kurt Mendelssohn believes that the pyramids have political significance. In *The Riddle of the Pyramids*, he points to physical evidence—for example, the chemical makeup of the mortar—that shows that the construction periods of at least some of the pyramids overlapped. This means that the pyramids could not all have been built consecutively, with each new pharaoh ordering and building his tomb as he ascended the throne. Also, some pharaohs, such as Sneferu, had more than one pyramid built. If the pyramid was to be his tomb, the pharaoh had no reason to build more than one.

Mendelssohn concludes that the pyramids were massive public works projects rather than tombs. During the First and Second Dynasties, Egypt was in disarray. People paid their allegiance less to the pharaoh than to their local tribal chieftain. Because the tribes continually warred with one another, the nation was in constant turmoil. In Mendelssohn's view people thought of themselves as members of clans or tribes. They did not think of themselves as Egyptians.

A Common Venture

The pyramids changed that. First, they employed a steady stream of unskilled labor. The workers went back to their villages, heroes of sorts for having had a hand in a project that brought glory to Egypt. Some of the inscriptions carved on the stone blocks by quarry workers—"Vigorous Gang," "Enduring Gang"—attest to a pride in their work and a camaraderie among the workers, strangers who had come from formerly competing tribes. Much of the granite used at Giza was transported from as far away as six hundred miles to the south—even though plenty of usable stone was available right across the Nile. Mendelssohn argues that this was a deliberate design by rulers to bring the northern and southern parts of the kingdom together in a common venture. Mendelssohn concludes:

> The pyramid project was creating a type of community which had never existed before. Tribal villagers were welded by common work into people with the consciousness of nationhood. It was probably for the first time that they thought of themselves first and foremost as Egyptians.

From this perspective, says Mendelssohn, some of the problems that beset the tomb theory recede into the background. It makes no difference whether or not anyone was ever entombed in the pyramids, for that was not their primary purpose. What is significant about the pyramids is that they helped to create a new form of social organization, the national state, that has survived intact throughout the world for thousands of years.

Of course, not all Egyptologists agree with Mendelssohn. William Simpson, an archaeologist at Boston's Museum of Fine Arts, would argue that Mendelssohn confuses cause and effect. The pyramids did not *cause* the emergence of the state. The state had to be organized and effective first, he says, before the massive pyramid project could be successfully undertaken.

A Bible in Stone

Sometime around 300 B.C., an Egyptian priest and historian named Manetho wrote: "There came up from the East, in a strange manner, men of an ignoble race" who conquered the Egyptians "without a battle." Statements such as this, made in connection with Egypt's early history, have led some pyramid scholars to believe that the pyramids were built not by the Egyptians but by the Israelites, God's so-called chosen people, led perhaps by Shem or the priest-king Melchizedek. These pyramid scholars share the belief that the Egyptians were not culturally and scientifically advanced enough to build the pyramids. The pyramids, they say, are so complex that the builders must have been divinely inspired, sent by God to build them as a form of biblical prophecy.

One of the earliest Western proponents of this theory was John Taylor, a London editor and gifted mathematician, who published *The Great Pyramid: Why Was It Built and Who Built It?* in 1859. His views were taken up in the mid-1800s by Piazzi Smythe, a professor who held the position of Astronomer Royal of Scotland. In recent years similar views have been expressed by Adam Rutherford, who, in a series of books, has called the Great Pyramid a "bible in stone."

In his 1928 book *The Witness of the Great Pyramid*, Basil Stewart stated the biblical theory. The Great Pyramid, he wrote,

> reveals a system of prophetic chronology which runs parallel with—and confirms—Biblical prophecy, forecasting events which history has proved correct in the past, are being confirmed to-day, and are due to take place in the immediate future.

"The Grand Gallery['s] . . . length coincides with the duration of the Gospel Age, from the death of Christ in 33 A.D. [until] Autumn of the year 1914 A.D., when . . . Christ will take to himself his mighty power."

John and Morton Edgar, *The Great Pyramid Passages and Chambers*

"Discoveries have been made which now make it impossible for any well-informed [person] to accept the . . . fundamental assumption on which this Biblical theory is based."

William Kingsland, *The Great Pyramid in Fact and in Theory*

In other words, just as the words of a poem or the images or design of a painting can symbolize a larger truth, so the Great Pyramid somehow embodies or illustrates the truths of the Bible. Taylor, Smythe, and their followers focused intently on the measurements of the Great Pyramid, trying to discover the units of measure the builders used. These units, occurring in regular patterns, suggest that each of the Pyramid's blocks, or perhaps the length of the Grand Gallery or the height of the King's Chamber, represented years since the Creation and embodied prophecies of biblical events, including the birth of Jesus. The person who found the key to the builders' system would hold the key to biblical prophecy.

Many skeptics, including Egyptologist William Kingsland, dispute the biblical theory. In their view the theory rests on highly laborious systems of measurement that can be bent to suit any theory, no matter how far-fetched. It also tends to rely on a literal interpretation of the Old Testament, according to which Adam and Eve were created in about 4000 B.C. "Whatever may have been the concealed mystery of the Pyramid," concludes Kingsland, "it was [not] intended that the mystery should require that every Passage and Chamber should be elaborately . . . measured up to thousandths of [an] . . . inch."

A Temple of Initiation

Some pyramid scholars see a link between the Great Pyramid and what are called the Egyptian Mysteries. The Egyptian Mysteries are the secret knowledge reputedly held by a small group called Initiates. The mysteries are passed along to new Initiates only after a long and arduous period of training. It is difficult to describe the nature of the knowledge; perhaps it can best be described as the laws and principles of the universe and an understanding of humanity's place in creation.

One writer who took this position was Helena P. Blavatsky. In her 1888 book *The Secret Doctrine,*

"Basically, we look at the Great Pyramid as the burial place for the king, and that is what it was designed for."

Dr. Edward Wente, Oriental Institute, University of Chicago

"Perhaps they served some religious or mystical purpose. We simply can't be sure."

John Cooney, director, Brooklyn Museum's Egypt collection

Blavatsky describes the Great Pyramid as "the everlasting record and the indestructible symbol of the Mysteries and Initiations on Earth." In an earlier book called *Isis Unveiled*, she writes that the Great Pyramid "symbolized the creative principle of Nature, and illustrated also the principles of geometry, mathematics, astronomy and astrology."

Secrets Revealed

According to Blavatsky and her followers, initiation rituals were conducted inside the Great Pyramid. The Pyramid, she writes, "was a temple of initiation where men rose towards the Gods and the Gods descended towards men." The empty sarcophagus in the King's Chamber was the centerpiece of many of these rituals. The new Initiate was laid in the sarcophagus for three days and three nights. There he had what today might be called an out-of-body experience—a sense that his spirit was rising above his body. He would awaken possessing the understanding of Thoth, the Egyptian god of wisdom. In the view of William Kingsland, the tradition of secret knowledge continued into the twentieth century. The secrets, he says, are known to twentieth-century Initiates, but they choose not to reveal what they know to the world at large. Kingsland concludes that if the Great Pyramid was built by Initiates for new Initiates, these builders drew on their understanding of profound and mysterious natural forces. If we understand those forces, Kingsland says, we would understand how and why the pyramids were built.

A related theory holds that the pyramids had a more specific role in preserving ancient Egyptian culture and beliefs. According to this view the Great Pyramid is a monument that embodies the doctrines of the ancient Egyptian texts called *The Book of the Dead*. These texts do not actually form a book. Rather, they are a collection of hieroglyphs and papyrus scrolls that have been found in Egyptian

According to Blavatsky, after spending three days and three nights in an empty sarcophagus, Initiates awakened possessing the understanding of Thoth, the Egyptian god of wisdom.

tombs and in mummy wrappings. The longest known specimen is a twenty-meter-long (nearly sixty feet) scroll found with a mummy that is now housed in the museum at Turin, Italy.

The texts, which the ancient Egyptians said came from Thoth, are a collection of funereal and religious writings. The Egyptians believed that the writings had great mystic power and that they were essential to protecting the souls of the dead. They helped guide the dead through their journey to the afterlife. One text, for example, reads:

> Of the Khu [spiritual soul] for whom this Book shall be recited, his soul shall come forth by day with the living, he shall have power among the gods, and it will make him irresistible for ever and ever. These gods shall go round about him, and shall acknowledge him. He shall be one of them.

Many writers, including W. Marshal Adams in *The Book of the Master*, argue that the Egyptians were eager to preserve the wisdom of *The Book of*

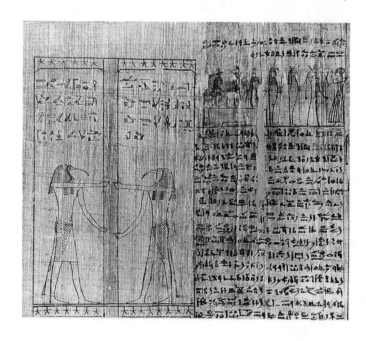

The Book of the Dead is actually a collection of hieroglyphs and papyrus scrolls found in tombs and mummy wrappings. This specimen shows an ibis-headed Thoth.

the Dead. They also wanted to withhold the book's secrets from those who were not initiated. They built the Great Pyramid—and perhaps other pyramids as well—to these ends. They relied on the Pyramid's measurements, the placement and angles of the passages, the size of the chambers, and the positioning of the blocks to transmit their knowledge to succeeding generations of Initiates. In this way the Great Pyramid became a lasting record of the scientific, technical, and philosophical achievements embodied in *The Book of the Dead.* The pyramids are thus a code that only a few select people are able to decipher.

Extraterrestrial Origins?

Some pyramid historians conclude that the pyramids must have an otherworldly origin. They believe that the ancient Egyptians did not have the tools or the technical knowledge to build such immense structures. Even if they did, they lacked the ability to build them with such absolute precision. These theorists, unlike the biblical theorists, do not conclude that the pyramids have a divine origin. Rather, they believe the pyramids were built by extraterrestrials—visitors from outer space.

One of the foremost of these theorists is Erich von Däniken. In his widely read book *Chariots of the Gods?*, von Däniken claims that many of the earth's wonders could have been built only by extraterrestrial beings with superior knowledge. He points out that the Great Pyramid sits almost squarely on the point at thirty degrees latitude and thirty degrees longitude. Along these lines the world's continents and oceans are divided into equal halves. Only a race with superior astronomical and navigational abilities could have chosen that as the spot for the Pyramid, he says. Von Däniken also argues that the Nile Valley did not have enough resources to feed the vast number of workers needed to build the pyramids. Additionally, the absence of soot from torches in the

"The only way the pyramid's planners could have picked its central position . . . would have been to survey Earth from space."

TV producers and authors Alan and Sally Landsburg, *In Search of Ancient Mysteries*

"Some people still feel that little green men in pink flying saucers came down and built the pyramids."

John Cooney, director, Brooklyn Museum's Egypt collection

pyramids' chambers and passageways raises the possibility that artificial lighting was used. Evidence such as this convinces von Däniken and his many followers that the pyramids must have been built by visitors from outer space.

Another writer who takes this position is Zecharia Sitchin, author of *The Earth Chronicles*, *The Stairway to Heaven*, and *The Wars of Gods and Men*. Central to Sitchin's theory are ancient Sumerian stories about the Anunnaki, "those who from Heaven to Earth came." These stories have generally been thought of as legends, but Sitchin wonders if they could be true—if the Anunnaki were visitors from another planet.

Sitchin argues that some thirteen thousand years ago, a deluge, or flood, destroyed the cities and

Do the pyramids have extraterrestrial origins? Because construction of the pyramids required great ingenuity, some historians conclude that they were built by visitors from outer space.

spaceports the Anunnaki had built in what is today Iraq. As the waters receded, they had to construct a new landing corridor for their craft. On the northeast they anchored it on the twin peaks of Mount Ararat. On the southwest they anchored it on the twin mountain peaks on the Sinai Peninsula. But on the northwest corner there was only desert. The Anunnaki, Sitchin concludes, built the two large pyramids at Giza to provide corresponding twin peaks in that corner. (The Third Pyramid, he says, was a scale model.) Now their arrow-shaped landing corridor was marked at each corner by matching twin peaks.

According to Sitchin all this happened around 9000 B.C., long before the advent of Egypt's Old Kingdom. No reliable evidence, says Sitchin, supports the claims of Egyptologists that the pyramids were built by pharaohs in later years. He believes, for example, that an inscription in the Great Pyramid bearing Khufu's name is fraudulent, added later by those bent on proving he was the builder. (It should be noted that Sitchin's and von Däniken's views are accepted by few historians and scientists.)

Which Theory Is True?

These are some of the most important theories that pyramid historians and archaeologists have offered to explain the purpose of the pyramids. These are not the only theories, however. During the nineteenth century, a time of great interest in Egypt and the pyramids, a number of competing theories emerged. These theories emphasize the mathematical regularities of the pyramids and raise the possibility that the pyramids were constructed as scientific tools to serve an assortment of purposes. These theories have persisted as the strongest competitors of the dominant tomb theory.

Three

Were the Pyramids Built as Scientific Instruments?

In the thirteenth century an Arab poet wrote about the pyramids: "A maddening desire to comprehend their meaning surges in the heart of the beholder." Poetry is one response to the majesty of the pyramids, profiled against the desert sky. Scientific investigation is another.

By all accounts Col. Richard Howard-Vyse, an officer in the British Guards, was not a poetic man. In 1836 he saw the pyramids at Giza during a moonlit camel ride. Although his response was not poetic, it reflected "a maddening desire to comprehend their meaning," he said. Determined to learn all he could about the Great Pyramid, he hired a civil engineer and a team of workers, and for nearly a year, "he sat down before [it] as a fortress to be besieged," as a friend later wrote.

For centuries the base of the Great Pyramid had been heaped high with debris—sand, trash, and fragments of rock. Howard-Vyse resolved to clear away these piles on the north side. His purpose was to do something that no other explorer had done, at least to anyone's knowledge: to get down to the very base of the Pyramid. There he would be able to take accurate measurements both of the Pyramid's circumference and of its height.

(Opposite page) Did the ancient Egyptians possess advanced knowledge about mathematics, geography, and astronomy? If so, were the pyramids used as scientific instruments?

Polished limestone casing stones once covered the craggy surface of the Great Pyramid, giving it a smooth, shiny appearance.

As the piles—many as high as fifty feet—were being carted away, the colonel must have felt gratified at the prospect of being the first person in centuries to see the foundation on which the Pyramid rested. But a startling discovery awaited him. For when the workers reached the lowest level, they uncovered two of the original polished-limestone casing stones, still positioned where the Pyramid's builders had placed them thousands of years before.

The discovery of the casing stones was important for at least two reasons. At that time archaeologists disagreed about whether the Pyramid had originally been covered by a limestone casing, which would have given the Pyramid a smooth and polished appearance. Howard-Vyse's discovery put that dispute to rest. More importantly, the blocks—which were five feet high, twelve feet long, and eight feet wide—were so finely polished and fit into their niches so tightly that it was now possible to correctly measure the precise slope of the Pyramid's sides, which angled up at a slope of 51 degrees, 52 minutes. With this information, Howard-Vyse was now able to calculate the exact height of the Pyramid, which would have been 485.5 feet with the crowning casing stone in position.

Howard-Vyse returned to England in 1840 and presented the results of his investigations in a two-volume book, *Operations Carried on at the Pyramids of Gizeh in 1837*. An accident, however, had taken some of the glow off his accomplishments. On the return journey he was shipping the sarcophagus of Menkure from the Third Pyramid back to the British Museum. Misfortune overtook the ship, and it sank in deep water off the coast of Spain. It has never been recovered.

Howard-Vyse was one of the earliest in a procession of explorers and archaeologists who measured nearly every detail of the pyramids. They were seeking in those measurements some clue to the pyramids' construction and to their purpose. As data accumulated, noteworthy patterns in the measurements began to emerge. These patterns led some investigators to wonder whether the pyramids were built to encode mathematical formulas, to model astronomical information, or to serve in some way as scientific instruments. If true, their theories would suggest that the ancient Egyptians possessed a level of ingenuity and technical know-how higher than had ever been suspected. They would also stand in opposition to later claims by the biblical theorists and writers such as Erich von Däniken that the pyramids must have an otherworldly origin.

A Mathematics Text in Stone

The imaginations of many nineteenth-century explorers and archaeologists, both professional and amateur, were fired by the mathematical regularities they saw in the pyramids, especially the Great Pyramid. Many were convinced, for example, that the Pyramid was constructed as a record in stone of *pi*, the mathematical concept usually represented by the Greek letter π. *Pi* is an important mathematical relationship, perhaps one of the most fundamental of all geometrical formulas. It is the relation between a circle's circumference and its diameter. For everyday purposes, the value assigned to *pi* is 3.14; a more precise value would be 3.14159265. Modern mathematicians armed with sophisticated computers have been unable to determine its exact value; this is because its decimal places seem to extend infinitely. What the number says is that the distance around any circle, its circumference, is slightly more than three times the distance across the circle, its diameter. *Pi* is also used to compute a circle's area. Its value does not depend on whether measurements are made in inches, miles, or some other unit. The length around a circle is always the circle's diameter multiplied by *pi*.

Preserving *Pi*

Historians had always assumed that the value of *pi* was discovered long after the pyramid age. The earliest known evidence that the ancient Egyptians knew *pi* had dated to around 1700 B.C. But when John Taylor, the London editor with a keen interest in mathematics, examined the measurements recorded in Richard Howard-Vyse's book, he reached a conclusion that he believed was inescapable: the builders of the Great Pyramid must have known the approximate value of *pi*. His conclusion was seconded by Piazzi Smythe and other investigators.

The principal calculation that led to this conclusion was that the height of the Great Pyramid is the same as the perimeter of the Pyramid's base divided by 2 *pi*. These investigators believed that this could not have happened by coincidence. They drew the conclusion that one of the underlying purposes of the Pyramid was to incorporate the value of *pi*, preserving it for later civilizations.

Not all investigators agree with these conclusions. In the *Atlas of Ancient Egypt*, John Baines and Jaromír Málek point out that the Egyptians

"In spite of brilliant constructional skill and superb workmanship, we have no evidence that the Egyptians of the Old Kingdom had more than the most rudimentary command of mathematics."

Kurt Mendelssohn, *The Riddle of the Pyramids*

"In mathematics they were advanced enough to have discovered . . . the function of π."

Peter Tompkins, *Secrets of the Great Pyramid*

could have incorporated *pi* accidentally. They might, for example, have measured distances not with rulers but by rolling a drum or a barrel and counting the number of revolutions. The length of each roll of the drum would be equal to the drum's circumference, so any measurement taken this way would preserve the *pi* relationship.

Other Mathematical Relationships

Several nineteenth-century investigators, including Taylor and Smythe, observed other mathematical relationships in the Great Pyramid. Some believe that the dimensions of the King's Chamber and the layout of the entire Giza complex showed that the builders understood the Pythagorean theorem thousands of years before Pythagoras, the Greek mathematician who explained the relationships among the sides of triangles. They pointed out that the area of each of the Pyramid's faces, or sides, was equal to the square of its height (the height multiplied by itself).

These explorers, led by Smythe, were also fascinated by the Pyramid's apparent units of measurement. They tried to show, for example, that the Pyramid's builders relied on a standard unit of measurement (they called it the pyramid inch) that corresponded to the dimensions of the earth or the length of the solar year. That is, each pyramid inch represented an equal portion of the earth's circumference or a day in the solar year.

As each explorer returned home laden with a new set of measurements, he was likely to construct yet another new theory that explained in mathematical terms why the pyramids were built. As newer, more accurate measurements became available, as they did, for instance, after Howard-Vyse's trip, old theories had to be revised or discarded.

What kinds of conclusions did these early writers draw from the mathematical patterns they found? One was that the Great Pyramid was built to

Did the pyramid builders understand the Pythagorean theorem thousands of years before it was explained by the Greek mathematician Pythagoras (pictured)?

serve as a kind of map of the earth's Northern Hemisphere. Taylor, for example, wrote in *The Great Pyramid: Why Was It Built and Who Built It?*:

> [The Egyptians] knew the earth was a sphere; and by observing the motion of the heavenly bodies over the Earth's surface, had ascertained its circumference, and were desirous of leaving behind them a record of the circumference as correct and imperishable as it was possible for them to construct.

Thus, the Great Pyramid's careful measurements could tell future investigators the exact circumference of the earth once they figured out the Pyramid's mathematical construction code.

A Map of the Earth

In the 1950s and 1960s, Livio Stecchini, a professor of the history of science, analyzed the Great Pyramid's measurements in a number of articles. He has summarized his views in an appendix to Peter Tompkins's book *Secrets of the Great Pyramid*. Like Taylor, Stecchini concludes that the Pyramid was intended as a map. He explains that the builders' design was to provide a mathematical map of the Northern Hemisphere. The apex, or highest point, of the Pyramid represented the North Pole; the perimeter of the base represented the earth's equator. The height of the Pyramid has to be multiplied by 2 *pi* to equal the equator because the Pyramid models only half of the earth. Stecchini also concludes that the Pyramid represents the Northern Hemisphere on a scale of 1 to 43,200. He believes that the Egyptians chose this scale because there are 86,400 seconds in twenty-four hours. Because the pyramid represents only one-half of the globe, half of the number of seconds was used as the scale. The point of these and similar calculations is that the Pyramid did not just happen, that it was not thrown together to satisfy the whim of a powerful pharaoh. It was the product of careful design and construc-

tion by builder-mathematicians whose goal was to create a lasting monument in stone for the knowledge they possessed.

A Surveyor's Landmark

In the 1880s Robert Ballard, an engineer, was riding a train in the neighborhood of the Giza Plateau. As he gazed at the pyramids through the window of the train, it suddenly struck him that with their clear profiles against the sky and their steadily changing relative positions, the pyramids would have made infallible surveyor's landmarks.

In *The Solution of the Pyramid Problem*, Ballard points out that the boundaries of the property belonging to the clans and villagers up and down the Nile were important. Most Egyptians made their living along the Nile Valley, and the valley's population density—the number of people per square mile—was high, as high as that of many modern, crowded countries. Each year, though, when the Nile rose from its banks, many property boundaries were washed out and had to be reestablished. In Ballard's view the range of pyramids down the west bank of the Nile provided a succession of reliable and stationary surveyor's landmarks that allowed the Egyptians to do just that.

The striking profiles of the Giza pyramids etched against the twilight sky seem to support the theory that the pyramids were built as infallible landmarks.

Ancient Egyptians use a length of rope to survey an area. Some historians believe that Egyptian surveyors could determine latitude and longitude based on the configuration of the three large Giza pyramids.

The pyramids would function in this way with the help of nothing more sophisticated than a stone and string. The string, pulled taut by the stone, would provide a straight line that could be aligned with any of the corners or peaks of the pyramids. Depending on where the surveyor stood, the three large pyramids in the distance had a unique configuration; the corner angle of one, for example, might line up directly on the peak of another. Based on that configuration and with the help of the string, the surveyor would know exactly where he was in relation to the earth's latitude and longitude. Ballard speculates that the Third Pyramid, unlike the other two, was encased in red granite to make it easier for a surveyor—who might be twenty or more miles away—to orient himself.

An Almanac

Pyramid historians have offered additional theories about scientific purposes the pyramids might have served. In his 1971 book *Secrets of the Great Pyramid*, Peter Tompkins makes this observation about the Egyptians' vital need for an accurate calendar:

With the present availability of cheap watches, radio signals and published almanacs, one is likely to underestimate the value to ancient people of a reliable system for telling the day, the season, the year, and, most important in Egypt, where the entire system of agriculture depended on the swamping of the arable land, the forthcoming flooding of the Nile.

Tompkins notes that the Egyptian peasant spent three-quarters of the year plowing, planting, and harvesting the fields along the Nile. For part of each year, though, the peasants had to move their families and belongings to higher ground, to escape the Nile's inundation. In modern societies people can time events like these with few problems. The ancient Egyptians, though, needed to have a reliable way to measure the passing of the seasons. Some pyramid scholars have argued that the pyramids formed a massive sundial that the Egyptians used to keep track of the seasons with near-absolute precision.

Measuring the Passage of Time

Nineteenth-century French astronomer Jean-Baptiste Biot was among the first to offer this theory. He wrote in *Research on Several Points of Egyptian Astronomy* that the Great Pyramid has, "since it first existed, functioned as an immense sundial which has marked annually the periods of the equinoxes . . . and those of the solstices." (An equinox is one of the two times each year when the sun crosses the equator, signaling the start of spring and fall. A solstice is one of the two times when the sun is farthest away from the equator, marking the start of summer and winter.) Later Piazzi Smythe observed that at the beginning of spring, the sun seems to perch squarely on the apex, or peak, of the Great Pyramid. Precisely at noon on the first day of spring, the shadow that covers the Pyramid's north face vanishes.

In his 1902 book *The Rational Almanac*, Moses B. Cotsworth developed the theory in more detail.

A detail of a tomb painting depicts the harvesting of wheat. The success of agriculture was crucial to the ancient Egyptians. Did the pyramids enable the Egyptians to measure the passing of the seasons and determine when to plow, plant, and harvest their crops?

"The ancient priests could have established by physical observation of the shadow on the flagstones, the precise length of a year to .24219 of a day."

Moses B. Cotsworth, *The Rational Almanac*

"[The pyramids] originated before anything like intellectual culture existed, have been constructed without thought of scientific method, and have owed their earliest forms to accident and caprice [whim]."

Professor F.A.P. Barnard, president in 1890s of Columbia College, New York City

He began by devising a model showing how the pyramids' shadows could be used to measure the length of the year. He observed that a square-based pyramid oriented to true north, as the Great Pyramid is, produces a succession of pointed shadows that accurately count off the days. To test his theory he visited the Giza Plateau in 1900. There he noticed that the paving stones on the pyramid's north side are positioned in a peculiar way. They are not lined up in rows but are staggered; the Pyramid's shadow during the winter months touches their joints in such a way that each stone marks off the passage of one day. A later explorer, David Davidson, observed that the same process would have occurred on the Pyramid's south face during the summer. The difference, though, was that the south face would not have cast a shadow. Rather, it would have reflected sunlight from its polished surface onto the ground. In this way the paving stones on the south side would have marked off the passage of days in the summer just as they did on the north side in winter. Scientists have made similar observations at other pyramids, such as those at Saqqara and Dahshûr.

Public Calendars

Cotsworth points out that the ancient Egyptians were not the only ones who used such a system to measure time. England, for example, has several massive grassy mounds, such as Old Sarum near Salisbury, that were shaped like step pyramids and were used for burial purposes. In ancient times these mounds were topped with poles that cast long shadows. These shadows were used to measure the passage of time. Dr. Lyle B. Borst, a professor of astronomy and physics, has shown that many cathedrals and churches in Europe are oriented to the points of the compass and have spires oriented toward solstices or equinoxes. Other monuments, such as England's Stonehenge, may have served similar purposes. As a group these structures suggest that ancient civilizations relied on their most prominent monuments to serve as public calendars.

An Astronomical Observatory

In the centuries after the pyramids were built, Arab historians wrote that the Great Pyramid was used as an astronomical observatory—a place where the positions and movements of heavenly bodies could be charted. They never made clear, though, how astronomers climbed the Pyramid's smooth sides or how they used its interior passages to make their observations.

In his 1883 book *The Great Pyramid: Observatory, Tomb, and Temple*, the astronomer Richard Proctor hit on a solution. He wondered if ancient astronomers completed their task *before* the Pyramid was finished. Proctor theorized that the Pyramid became a temporary observatory when the stone course at the top of the Grand Gallery was reached. The gallery would give out onto a level platform where astronomers were free to work. That platform, at the fiftieth stone course, would have been exactly half the area of the Pyramid's base. Proctor did not know, however, what significance this might have.

Stonehenge, located in England, may have enabled ancient peoples to measure the passing of time.

56

Proctor demonstrates in great detail how the ancient Egyptians oriented the Great Pyramid precisely to the north. They began, he says, by observing the movements of the stars around the North Star, whose position is fixed. In this way they could locate true north. As they built the Great Pyramid, Proctor says, they made sure that the descending passage pointed directly at the North Star. This gave the passage a 26-degree angle; the ascending passage rises at precisely the same 26-degree angle.

Proctor's theory also offers a plausible explanation for the use of the Grand Gallery. He explains that an ancient astronomer who wanted an observa-

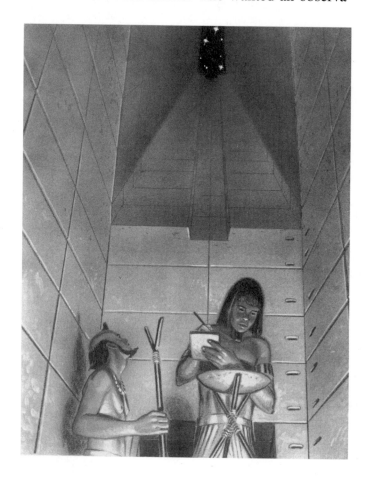

An artist's conception of how the Grand Gallery might have been used as an observatory before the Great Pyramid was completed.

tion slot could not have done better than the gallery. It is high up in the Pyramid with perfectly aligned walls. It is narrow at the top, and it is positioned so that the opening that would have been at the top before the Pyramid was completed is precisely divided in half by a meridian—that is, by one of the imaginary circles around the earth that pass through the poles, like the longitudinal circles drawn on a globe. Looking up from the bottom of the gallery, the astronomer could watch the stars as they passed and note precisely when each crossed the meridian. This is little different from what a modern astronomer does in an observatory.

Proctor provides many details to support his theory. He explains, for example, how the ancient astronomers could have timed the passing of a star. They may have placed a pool of water where the ascending and descending passages meet. At the instant a star passed the meridian, it would be reflected in the pool of water. Both moments before and moments later, its light would bounce off the walls of the narrow passages and be unobservable. Peter Tompkins notes that the U.S. Naval Observatory in Washington, D.C., uses almost exactly the same system, timing stars from their momentary reflections in a pool of mercury.

Able Astronomers

It is clear that the ancient Egyptians were able astronomers. Somehow they amassed an extraordinary amount of astronomical information, all without benefit of telescopes. Their ability, writes Harvard professor George Sarton,

> is proved not only by their calendars, tables of star culminations [when they were directly overhead], and tables of star risings, but also by some of their instruments such as ingenious sundials or the combination of a plumb line with a forked rod that enabled them to determine the azimuth [arc] of a star.

"The Great Pyramid . . . was designed on the basis of a hermetic geometry known only to a restricted group of initiates."

Peter Tompkins, *Secrets of the Great Pyramid*

"The Washington Monument proves as much about history, astronomy, and numerology as does the Great Pyramid— if you have the patience and time to waste on silly projects."

Magician James Randi, *Flim Flam*

Surveyors who worked for the French general Napoleon Bonaparte theorized that the Great Pyramid was built as a geodetic landmark.

It is certainly possible that the pyramids were important tools in the hands of the Egyptian astronomers.

Geographical Landmarks

The ancient Egyptians were not only capable astronomers; they were just as adept at geodesy. Geodesy is a branch of geography that uses astronomy and surveying methods to establish landmarks and to determine the dimensions of the earth. Some pyramid historians believe that the pyramids could have been built as geodetic landmarks.

The first modern surveyors to suspect that the Great Pyramid served such a purpose worked for Napoleon Bonaparte, the French general who conquered Egypt in 1798. They discovered that the meridian that cuts the pyramid in half from north to south also divides the delta region at the mouth of the Nile into two equal halves. They also discovered that if the Pyramid's diagonals—the X that would join the corners of its base—were extended, they would almost perfectly enclose the delta region. The surveyors concluded that the Pyramid could not have been positioned this way by accident. But the reason for this positioning remains unclear.

Livio Stecchini has provided some answers. In studying the Egyptians' knowledge of geodesy, he has gathered evidence showing that as far back as 3000 B.C. the Egyptians were able to measure latitude and longitude within a few hundred feet. Ancient texts also show that they knew the circumference of the earth and had accurately surmised the dimensions of their country. According to Stecchini, they used the Great Pyramid as a key geodetic landmark. Around it they developed a system of geography that enabled them to locate any natural landmark in that part of the world relative to the Pyramid. As their knowledge spread to other countries, Egypt and the Pyramid became the geodetic center of the known world around the Mediterranean. Other countries, Stecchini says, located their cities and monuments in relation to Egypt and the meridian that divided the country in half.

Conflicting Theories

As new information about the pyramids became available in the nineteenth and twentieth centuries, archaeologists and historians offered new explanations for why the pyramids were built. Despite the many intriguing ideas that have been proposed, most scientists and historians remain convinced that the pyramids' chief purpose was to be tombs—although they may have had secondary purposes as scientific tools. Believing this issue settled, many focus their attention on the second question that has teased archaeologists and visitors for centuries: How were the pyramids built?

Four

How Were the Pyramids Built?

(Opposite page) The construction of the massive pyramids was an incredible technical feat. Even today, the question lingers: How were the pyramids built? Pictured is an artist's conception of Egyptians putting stones in place using a series of ropes and logs.

Sometime around 450 B.C., the Greek historian Herodotus paid a visit to the Egyptian pyramids. At the time, most of the pyramids were already more than two thousand years old—about as ancient to Herodotus as Herodotus is to readers today.

The fruit of the historian's visit was one of the earliest known accounts of the Great Pyramid. Relying on information he obtained from Egyptian priests living in the area, Herodotus wrote in his *History:*

> [Cheops] closed the temples, and forbade the Egyptians to offer sacrifices, compelling them instead to labor, one and all, in his service. Some were required to drag blocks of stone down to the Nile from the quarries in the Arabian range of hills; others received the blocks after they had been conveyed in boats across the river, and drew them to the range of hills called the Libyan. One hundred thousand men labored constantly, and were relieved every three months by a fresh lot. It took ten years' oppression of the people to make the causeway for the conveyance of the stones. . . . The Pyramid itself was twenty years in building.

Herodotus also described how the Great Pyramid was constructed:

The pyramid was built in steps. . . . After laying the stones for the base, they raised the remaining stones to their places by means of machines formed of short wooden planks. The first machine raised them from the ground to the top of the first step. On this there was another machine, which received the stone upon its arrival, and conveyed it to the second step, whence a third machine advanced it still higher. Either they had as many machines as there were steps in the pyramid, or possibly they had but a single machine, which, being easily moved, was transferred from tier to tier.

Herodotus even had something to say about provisions for the workers:

There is an inscription in Egyptian characters on the pyramid which records the quantity of radishes, onions, and garlic consumed by the laborers who constructed it.

Herodotus seems to answer some questions about how the Great Pyramid was built. The problem, though, is that his account is filled with factual errors and inconsistencies. He says, for example, that it took a total of thirty years to build a causeway and the Pyramid. But the best records indicate that Khufu's (Cheops's) reign lasted only twenty-three years. In addition, to have built a machine, or mechanical device, on each tier, the builders would have needed forests of wood—a scarce commodity in the deserts of Egypt. And if they had moved a single machine for each tier, the construction process would have been painfully slow, probably longer than Khufu's reign. Because of troubling inconsistencies like these, modern historians are not inclined to accept Herodotus's account as true, at least in all its details.

A Monumental Task

If Herodotus's account cannot be accepted, what *is* known about the construction of the Great Pyramid—still the largest stone building in the world? Even with the help of modern machinery, modern

After visiting the Egyptian pyramids around 450 B.C., the Greek historian Herodotus wrote one of the earliest known accounts of the Great Pyramid.

engineers and contractors might well find it a daunting task to build anything as big. How did the ancient Egyptians—without wheels, pulleys, or draft horses—manage to assemble the most enduring of the ancient world's Seven Wonders?

The ancient Egyptians left no written record describing how they built the pyramids. Modern archaeologists have had to rely on the tools of their own trade to fill in the gap. When they have drawn conclusions about the construction process, they have had to rely on various sorts of evidence:

• *Fragments of other pyramids:* Pyramids that were left incomplete give archaeologists a picture of the early stages of the building process for other pyramids.

• *Objects found at pyramid sites:* Archaeologists look for remains of tools and scraps of metal that suggest the kinds of tools the builders used.

The image of an ancient Egyptian carpenter with tool in hand has been preserved for modern study. Such artwork helps archaeologists piece together the story of how the pyramids were built.

• *Artwork:* Artwork found both in pyramids and at other construction sites often depicts construction in progress, showing both tools and methods. Archaeologists can infer that similar methods were used elsewhere.

• *Deduction:* Sometimes archaeologists have no direct evidence that supports a theory. They can, however, deduce how something might have been done, based on what they know about available tools, the nature of the building site, and common sense.

As the pyramids have been examined, bits and pieces of evidence have accumulated. Sometimes the evidence is inconclusive, and archaeologists disagree about what the details mean. But over the past century and a half, they believe that they have largely solved the puzzle. The possibility remains, however, that new evidence will come to light, requiring them to reexamine their conclusions and perhaps offer new ones.

Quarrying the Stone

A visitor to the pyramids is likely to first wonder where the stone came from and how the builders transported it to the building site.

The pyramids are made mostly of limestone. This limestone was quarried from various sites in the vicinity of Cairo. Archaeologists agree that because limestone is relatively soft, the Egyptians could cut it with their copper tools. Greater problems were posed by the much harder granite stones that were used, for example, in the King's Chamber and the Grand Gallery. These stones came from quarries hundreds of miles to the south, near Aswan. Copper tools are not hard enough to cut granite. In the nineteenth century archaeologist Sir Flinders Petrie found fragments of saws and drills. He speculated that these were tipped with diamond or some other hard jewel stone. Tools such as these could have been used to cut and shape the stone.

"How and with what were the stone blocks cut out of the quarries? . . . None of the explanations stands up to a critical examination."

Erich von Däniken, *Chariots of the Gods?*

"The stone-cutting was accomplished not with lasers, but with copper chisels and saws."

Ronald Story, *Guardians of the Universe?*

Erecting the pyramids might have looked something like this. Because hauling the stones required concentrated manpower, workers teamed up to drag the stones into position.

Archaeologists have also discovered hammers made of dolerite, itself a hard basalt rock, at ancient Egyptian construction and quarry sites. In his 1978 book *Ancient Egypt*, historian Lionel Casson speculates that workers could have used these hammers to chip slots in the stone. They could then have jammed wooden wedges into the slots. These wedges would be soaked with water, and when they expanded, pieces of the rock would break off. In *The Pyramids of Egypt*, archaeologist I.E.S. Edwards says that the stone could have been entirely chipped out with these hammers. As evidence, he points to another quarry site, where a massive obelisk, or pillar, was being chipped out of the rock in this way. The project was abandoned, apparently because a flaw was found in the obelisk.

Once the stones were cut and shaped, they were moved from the quarry site on a system of log rollers. One side of the stone would be smooth; that side would be tipped down onto the rollers. Workers would roll the stone to a ramp, where teams of workers using ropes would drag it to a wooden sledge. This sledge in turn would be used to drag the stone to a barge on the Nile, which would float the stone to the building site. The stone would be dragged on a similar ramp from the river's edge up to where it was needed. A process similar to this is illustrated in a detailed mural in a Twelfth Dynasty tomb. There is no reason to believe that Fourth Dynasty builders could not have used similar methods.

Preparing the Site

Meanwhile, the pharaoh's architects selected a site for the Pyramid. Khufu's architects, about whom little is known, selected a rocky knoll that rose from the desert floor west of Giza. They marked out the site so that the Pyramid's base would form a perfect square. Using their knowledge of astronomy, they oriented the Pyramid so that its sides would squarely face the four cardinal compass points—north, south, east, and west. Work gangs cut steplike terraces out of the rock. These terraces formed the foundation on which the Pyramid would be built.

A question that arises is how the builders were able to make the foundation so level. One corner of the thirteen-acre site is only a half inch higher than the opposite corner, and even that small difference may be the result of earth movements. As Ahmed Fakhry points out in *The Pyramids*, most archaeologists believe the Egyptians accomplished this by building a water-filled trench around the site. The water would stand at a uniform level. A string would be stretched between two sticks of equal length, the sticks held so that they just touched the water on opposite sides of the site. Measuring rods would be positioned at points along the string to ensure that when the ground was leveled, it was precisely parallel to the string.

Constructing the Pyramid

According to Herodotus, one hundred thousand slave laborers were needed for the monumental job of actually constructing the Great Pyramid and the complex of buildings surrounding it. Most historians today, however, believe that he was taken in by the exaggerations of his local guides. Casson estimates that only about four thousand workers were needed at one time. He confirms the estimate of Petrie, who put the number between thirty-six hundred and four thousand. Petrie based this estimate on evidence of the physical accommodations provided for the workers; in particular, the huts in which they lived.

Although most historians agree on roughly the number of workers, they do not agree about whether the laborers were slaves. In *The Great Pyramid in Fact and in Theory*, William Kingsland says that they probably were slaves. Casson, however, says that the laborers were free citizens. The Egyptians believed in the divinity of the pharaoh. A laborer or stonemason might very well have been proud to take part in a pyramid's construction. No records from the time answer this question.

Constructing a single public building in ancient Egypt required many laborers (pictured). Constructing the Great Pyramid was a much greater task; historians today believe that up to four thousand workers were needed at one time.

The central question for visitors to the pyramids has always been how the workers raised the stone blocks to their positions, some of them hundreds of feet above the pyramid's base. In the Great Pyramid, these stones average five thousand pounds. Herodotus wrote about wooden machines—presumably some kind of stationary lever—that would raise each block from course to course. Today, however, nearly every archaeologist rejects this notion. They agree that a system of ramps was built around the pyramid as it went up. As proof, they point to the unfinished pyramid of Sekhem-khet, near Saqqara. Here they uncovered the beginnings of a pyramid, with a descending passage and a burial chamber underneath. Still attached to the sides are the ramps the builders used until the project was abandoned.

Building these ramps and, later, carting them away, would have been a task almost as big as building the pyramid itself. The ramps were made of rock, sand, and rubble, requiring brick retaining walls to keep them in place. As the pyramid grew, so did the ramps. One can only imagine the extraordinary amount of labor involved as teams of ten to twenty workers, using ropes, sledges, and crowbars, wrestled the blocks, one by one, up the steep slopes of the ramps.

Arguments Against the Ramp Theory

While some version of the ramp theory is widely accepted, archaeologists are by no means unanimous. In his book *Mechanical Triumphs of the Ancient Egyptians*, Francis Barber finds weaknesses in the ramp theories. He points out that for any ramp to have a manageable slope, it would have to begin hundreds of feet away from the pyramid. To extend the ramps to the top of the pyramid, builders would have needed *four times* the volume of stone used in the pyramid. In effect, according to Barber, the ramp was a greater marvel than the Great Pyramid itself!

An illustration shows how laborers may have used mechanical wooden levers to put stones in position.

Arguments such as these have led some pyramid scholars to propose alternative methods of construction. In an article in *Natural History*, engineer Olaf Tellefsen suggested that the Egyptians used something like the machine Herodotus mentioned. This machine would consist of a wooden arm. The arm would be balanced with counterweights on a fulcrum, or support, which would be affixed to wooden skids. Stones could be lifted to their positions without the need for ramps. No evidence supports Tellefsen's suggestion, but it serves as a reminder that the Egyptians may have used mechanical contrivances about which nothing is known today.

While archaeologists generally agree about the overall method—that is, that the builders relied on ramps—they do not always agree about details. One question, for instance, is whether the polished casing stones were put in place as the Great Pyramid went up or whether they were added from the top down as the ramps were removed. Petrie concluded that they were added from the top down; Fakhry thinks it is more reasonable to conclude that they were added from the bottom up. A second issue concerns how the stones were placed before the mortar between them dried. Fakhry says that workers carefully smoothed the sides of each stone before putting it in place "with a thin layer of mortar." Kingsland, however, points out that two-ton stones were not simply dropped into place. In general, he says, the layers of mortar were very thin and would have dried before a stone could have been jockeyed into place. This leads him to wonder how the builders were able to achieve the precise, tight joints between stones. These are good examples of the many unanswered questions that have long teased pyramid scholars trying to understand Egyptian building methods.

Interior Construction

Most pyramids have interior passages and burial chambers similar to those found in the Great

"The pyramid was built around 2500 B.C., by which time Egyptian technology was comfortably equal to the demands."

Francis Hitching, Royal Archaeological Institute

"There are many problems connected with the technology of the pyramid builders and no genuine solutions."

Erich von Däniken, *Chariots of the Gods?*

Pyramid. But archaeologists have always taken special interest in the Great Pyramid's interior. They believe that its system of passageways and chambers indicates that the building plan changed. They believe that the original plan was for a much smaller pyramid. One archaeologist who holds this view is Ludwig Borchardt, founder of the German Institute of Archaeology in Cairo. In a series of books published in German, Borchardt says that the pit at the bottom of the descending passage was the original burial chamber. It was left incomplete because Khufu's ambitions grew. He ordered a larger pyramid, one with a chamber higher up—what is today called the Queen's Chamber. In *Mountains of Pharaohs*, Leonard Cottrell argues that the plan was changed even further, for the builders left the Queen's Chamber unfinished. The Pyramid's final design incorporated the King's Chamber at a still higher level.

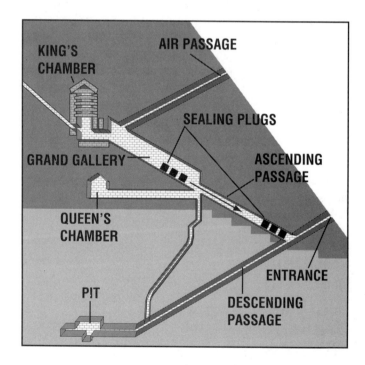

The labyrinth-like interior of the Great Pyramid.

The King's Chamber is one of the Great Pyramid's engineering marvels. Its roof is made of enormous granite slabs. These are arranged in a pagoda-like fashion to create five stress-relieving compartments. Some of the slabs have cracked, but they continue to firmly support the tons of stonework that press on them from above. The quarry marks on these stones refer to the seventeenth year of Khufu's reign, suggesting that the Pyramid was completed to this level by that point in his reign. These markings are the only place inside the Pyramid where Khufu's name appears.

The Grand Gallery

Archaeologists have long been puzzled by the Grand Gallery, which begins midway up the ascending passage and ends just outside the King's Chamber. They marvel at the precision with which its massive granite blocks are aligned. From post holes and other markings they have concluded that at least one purpose the gallery served was to help block the ascending passage. Most agree that the granite plugs Al Mamun encountered in the ninth century were originally placed inside the gallery as it was being built. They were held in place by wooden beams. When the beams were removed, the plugs slid down the gallery and into the ascending passage, blocking the way to the King's Chamber for would-be tomb robbers. The workers then escaped through a kind of well shaft that runs from the bottom of the gallery to the descending passage. Borchardt, however, rejects this theory, saying that the stone plugs would have been an "undignified obstacle" for the pharaoh's funeral cortege. Also, the theory does not explain what happened to the wooden beams, which would have been left inside but have never been found.

Archaeologists have also long admired the extreme precision of the descending passage. Petrie found that its alignment never varies by more than a quarter of an inch. Richard Proctor, the astronomer who concluded that the Great Pyramid was built as an observatory, offers an explanation. In his view the astronomers who designed the Pyramid wanted to make sure that it was perfectly oriented toward the North Star. They did this by first tunneling the descending passage, from the bottom, keeping it aligned as a kind of pointer. Proctor believes that as the Pyramid's first courses were laid, workers created the descending passage by tunneling *upward* through them. This would enable them to keep the descending passage precisely aligned.

Proctor goes on to explain the role of the ascending passage. He points out that when the descending passage exited the side of the Pyramid at the tenth course, its usefulness for orienting the Pyramid was at an end. The builders, though, had found a way to continue to use the North Star to orient the Pyramid. They plugged the descending passage and filled it part way with water. This would explain how the builders ensured that the joints of the stone in the passage were so precise, almost airtight. The North Star would reflect off this pool of water at the point where the descending and ascending passages meet. By tunneling upward from the descending passage at precisely the same angle—26 degrees—the builders could orient at least the next twenty or more courses using the North Star's reflection. This precise orientation was necessary, says Proctor, to make sure the Grand Gallery was correctly positioned and angled. Otherwise, it would have no use as an astronomical observatory.

Theories Abound

No direct evidence—historical accounts or wall paintings, for example—supports Proctor's claims other than the facts of the Pyramid itself: the angle of the passages, their straightness, the fine precision of the passages' joints, and the precise orientation of the Pyramid. It is unlikely that his theory, and its implications for the way the Pyramid was con-

structed, will ever be proved or disproved. It stands as an intriguing example of the many theories that surround not only the purpose of the pyramids, but also their method of construction.

Visitors to the Egyptian pyramids agree on one thing: no verbal description can convey the size and grandeur of the sight. In trying, though, Fakhry points out that if all the stone in the Great Pyramid were cut into one-square-foot blocks and laid end to end, the blocks would reach two-thirds of the way around the earth's equator. Comparisons such as this still pale beside the august reality of the pyramids. They fail to account for the pyramids' long-lasting mystique.

While archaeologists continue to debate how and why the pyramids were built, few would disagree that their beauty is timeless.

Five

Are the Pyramids Cursed?

In 1992 archaeologists were excavating some of the small tombs and mastabas near the Giza pyramids. They came up upon the tomb of an ancient Egyptian official named Pet-et-ty. Entombed with the official was his wife, Nesey-seker.

What was unusual about the tomb was that it contained two curses. Written on the wall in hieroglyphs, Pet-et-ty's curse calls on crocodiles, lions, and hippopotamuses to devour any one who dares to violate the tomb. Nesey-seker's curse enlists the same animals, but adds scorpions and snakes to the list. Clearly, the two did not want their tomb to be disturbed, and for forty-six hundred years they got their wish.

Strange Occurrences

Until October 1992. Then, according to Mansour Bauriak, an Egyptian antiquities inspector in charge of the excavations, when Pet-et-ty and Nesey-seker's tomb was disturbed, things started to go wrong. One inspector's home was destroyed by an earthquake; an experienced photographer was injured when his ladder collapsed in Pet-et-ty's burial chamber; a train carrying material away from the site derailed; and Zahi Hawass, Egypt's chief antiquities official, suffered a near-fatal heart attack.

(Opposite page) Mysterious bouts of illness and fatigue plague those who venture into the dark recesses of an Egyptian tomb. Is there a scientific explanation, or are the pyramids cursed?

Though Hawass blames the heart attack on overwork, his colleagues are not so sure.

Some of them blame it on the curses.

Mysterious Deaths

For centuries, many people have believed that the ancient pharaohs or their priests cursed the royal tombs, so that if anyone dared disturb them—and thus put the pharaohs' afterlife at risk—they would be punished. However, the *evidence* for the pharaoh's mysterious curse is anecdotal. That is, the evidence consists entirely of stories of deaths, illnesses, and disasters that have befallen those who have worked on the pyramids or, in some instances, have just visited them. So far no one has been able to prove whether the many tragic events associated with the pyramids are coincidences, exaggerations, or actually caused in some way by the ancient pharaohs.

Among the most dramatic incidents connected to a pyramid were the deaths of Sir Flinders Petrie and his colleague, Professor George Reisner, in 1942. Like Petrie, Reisner was a prominent Egyptologist. He had discovered the tomb of Khufu's mother, and he made radio history when he shared his knowledge of the Great Pyramid with the world by broadcasting from inside the King's Chamber in 1939. This was the first time such a broadcasting feat had been attempted. In the spring of 1942 he was inside the Pyramid when he collapsed. He was dragged from the Pyramid, paralyzed, and died a short time later. Then in July of the same year, Petrie was on his way home to England when he, too, suddenly and inexplicably died.

These are not the only deaths connected with the pharaohs' tombs. In 1823 the Italian explorer Giovanni Belzoni died of a mysterious disease after excavating the tomb of Seti I, a pharaoh from the Nineteenth Dynasty. In 1858 four European tourists who had visited the pyramids at Giza died within days of

The coffin of King Tutankhamen, who ruled from 1358 to 1349 B.C. A tablet in his tomb read, "Death will slay with his wings whoever disturbs the peace of the pharaoh."

one another. The death certificates listed various fevers as the cause. But doctors later testified that autopsy results had been falsified and that they could not give a medical explanation for the deaths.

At the time these deaths did not attract much attention. Speculation that the pharaohs' tombs were cursed became widespread in the popular press only after archaeologists in 1922 opened the tomb of King Tutankhamen, who ruled from 1358 to 1349 B.C. Historically he was not an important pharaoh, but "King Tut" has become a household name because of the magnificent treasures found in his sealed tomb, which was not a pyramid. According to Philipp Vandenberg in *The Curse of the Pharaohs,* at least three dozen scientists, archaeologists, and pyramid scholars died under mysterious circumstances—usually from fever or so-called circulatory collapse—after working on Tutankhamen's tomb or its artifacts. Many of these people worked at the tomb when it was first opened, including the British amateur Egyptologist Lord Carnarvon, who funded the venture. Supposedly, the crew, led by Carnarvon's partner Howard Carter, found a tablet in the tomb, inscribed: "Death will slay with his wings whoever disturbs the peace of the pharaoh." If the tablet was found, it was lost or broken. No trace of it remains in Tutankhamen's treasure trove.

This ornate necklace was among the treasures found in King Tut's tomb. At least three dozen people who worked on the tomb or its artifacts died suddenly and mysteriously.

Nevertheless, many people believe that Tutankhamen invoked such a curse and the many deaths linked to his tomb prove that he was as good as his word.

The Search for Explanations

One way to explain these mysterious deaths is to say that they were mere coincidence. In time, everyone is mortal, including archaeologists. By themselves, the deaths of a number of archaeologists who worked in a given pyramid or tomb mean nothing.

But many people worry that they are not coincidence. Some explain the deaths as proof of an ancient curse. How would such a curse work? Some say it is possible for a person—perhaps one trained as a religious mystic—to influence the course of another's life, even across many centuries. As Vandenberg points out, many twentieth-century psychologists, while not saying there are curses, argue that there are life rhythms that conceivably are subject to some sort of outside control. Those who can tap into these life rhythms can communicate telepathically, predict the future, and perform similar feats that run counter to reason. One of these feats might be to influence the health and well being of people in the future.

Scientists, however, have searched for other, more down-to-earth causes for the fevers, rashes, and other ailments that seem to have afflicted many people who have visited the pyramids and other archaeological sites in Egypt. Possible explanations they have found include fungi, bacteria, poisons, and radiation.

According to one theory some of these ailments might have been caused by a fungus often found in bat excrement. This fungus has been observed at archaeological sites around the world and is common in the Egyptian tombs. One disorder caused by the fungus often found in the tombs is called the

A decomposing mummy may provide the perfect breeding ground for harmful bacteria. If pyramids were in fact tombs containing mummies, this could explain the strange illnesses plaguing visitors.

Coptic itch. It produces skin rashes and breathing difficulties, similar to pneumonia. Several of the deaths connected to the pharaohs' tombs have been caused by pneumonia-like symptoms. Arthur Mace, a well-known archaeologist, reported that the walls of Tutankhamen's tomb were covered with a strange fungus.

Ezzeddin Taha, a Cairo doctor and biologist, announced in 1962 that he had found proof that such fungi could survive in tombs as long as four thousand years. He believed that antibiotics could combat the effect of the fungus and end the so-called curse of the pharaohs. Indeed, antibiotics saved the life of John Wiles. Wiles, a South African geologist, was studying the possibility of using bat excrement found in caves and tombs as a fertilizer. During his research in Rhodesian caves, he suddenly came down with high fever, indigestion, and aching muscles. Doctors concluded that it was the fungus causing his symptoms and used antibiotics to cure him.

Another theory is that some sort of bacteria that thrives in underground environments has made visitors become ill and die. Since the pyramids are presumed to have been tombs, they contained bodies, food, plants, and other formerly living substances. Despite the Egyptians' skill at mummification, some of these substances would have decayed. Decaying matter is a perfect breeding ground for bacteria.

Poison

A third possibility is that the people who died were exposed to poisons produced by herbs, plants, or poisonous animals such as snakes or scorpions. Any of these could lead to weakness, headaches, digestive upsets, hallucinations, insomnia, fevers—many of the symptoms pyramid workers complained of. They could also lead to death. Poisonous substances might be in the tombs accidentally, or they might have been purposely put there.

The ancient Egyptians were familiar with a variety of naturally occurring poisons, including nerve gas, reports Philipp Vandenberg. Egyptian priests had expert knowledge of drugs found in plants, minerals, animals, and insects. They commonly used substances such as tree resins, hemlock, and the poisons found in scorpion and certain frogs. They used them for curing illnesses, preserving foods and corpses, and poisoning enemies. Menes, the first pharaoh, had a garden containing poisonous plants, which he studied and experimented with. Cleopatra also was said to be knowledgeable about poisons. Poisons such as arsenic and aconite have been found mixed with the paints on the walls of some tombs. These may have simply been part of the paint formula. But some experts think the priests deliberately incorporated these poisons to harm anyone who invaded the tombs.

Cleopatra knew about poisons and how they could induce illness and even death.

"The curse of the pharaohs remains a phenomenon that has as yet no final explanation."

Philipp Vandenberg, *The Curse of the Pharaohs*

"I simply don't believe it [the curse of the pharaohs]."

Dr. Gamal Mehrez, Egyptian Museum of Cairo

Chemists have shown that many toxins, or poisons, are able to survive over thousands of years, especially when tightly sealed away from the deteriorating effects of air and light, as they would have been in the tombs. Some of the long-lasting toxins they studied can produce the symptoms that have overtaken many of those who worked in the pyramids. It is possible that these poisons were planted in the pyramids, where they lay in wait for thousands of years to wreak havoc on those who would presume to disturb the pharaohs' rest.

Radiation

Many of the symptoms that overtook pyramid workers, including extreme fatigue and circulatory collapse, are consistent with radiation poisoning. One scientist who has noted this is physicist Luis Bulgarini. Vandenberg quotes Bulgarini: "I believe that the ancient Egyptians understood the laws of atomic decay. Their priests and wise men were familiar with uranium." The pharaoh's curse, in other words, might be uranium placed in the floors and walls of the pyramids' chambers, where its deadly effects would eventually overtake intruders. Nobel Prize-winning scientist Luis W. Alvarez, however, does not think the pharaohs had to deliberately place uranium in the tombs. His research suggests that the pyramids somehow have strange and unknown effects on cosmic radiation, that is, the radiation that bombards the earth from the sun. It is possible that ancient Egyptian scientists knew this and used it to take vengeance on anyone who invaded the pyramids.

While it is possible that many of the deaths associated with the pharaoh's curse may have been caused by radiation, poisoning, bacteria, or fungi, the question that remains open is whether the ancient Egyptians understood these processes and used them to deliberately booby-trap tombs. Unfortunately, information about what they knew is scanty. It is clear that the ancient Egyptian priests used every means in their power to protect the bodies placed in the tombs from decay, grave robbers, and treasure seekers. And scraps of information found on clay tablets and parchments suggest that they might have enlisted the help of science to keep out intruders.

Pyramid Power?

In contrast to the curse that many attribute to the pyramids, others believe that they may have a mysterious beneficial power. Some, for example, believe that the pyramid form can speed up the process of mummification. A French radiologist named Jean

Some people believe that the pyramid form is associated with unusual powers.

According to French radiologist Jean Martial and others, the pyramid shape preserves and renews food and other items.

Martial conducted experiments in the 1950s that demonstrate, he said, that organic matter placed inside pyramids did not mold or decay but dried out, much as a mummy does. This process not only helped the ancient Egyptians preserve the bodies of their kings, but, some believe, could be used today to preserve food.

Others claim that the pyramid form has other remarkable powers. In 1959 a Czechoslovakian engineer named Karel Drbal placed a used razor blade inside a scale model of the Great Pyramid and oriented the pyramid to the true north. He claims that the edges of the blade recovered their sharpness; he even holds a patent in Czechoslovakia for Cheop's Pyramid Razor Blade Sharpener. He theorizes that the pyramid may accumulate cosmic rays or some other form of energy that returns the crystals of the blade's edge to their original form. Other researchers have claimed that milk stored in pyramidal, or pyramid-shaped containers stays fresh indefinitely without refrigeration.

"Pyramid power" was popularized in the 1970s and 1980s through the publicity gained by people like Drbal. It remains for many a staple of New Age beliefs and a trend among those who believe in paranormal forces and who argue that traditional science cannot explain all the forces that influence people's lives.

When Zahi Hawass (the Egyptian antiquities official who suffered a heart attack) was giving a lecture tour at American colleges, he was disconcerted at one college by a row of students who sat with plastic pyramids on their heads. They were meditating, they said, using the claimed power of the pyramid to focus their thoughts. Some people live in pyramid-shaped houses, believing that the form of the house can work magical effects in their lives. Dr. I.E.S. Edwards, retired Egyptian antiquities curator at the British Museum, refers to those who believe in the mystical power of pyramids as "pyramidiots." He may be right, but even in a technological age people look for unseen forces to explain life's mysteries. It seems inevitable that some would turn to the ancient Egyptians, who were capable of humbling modern science by building the world's most enduring monuments to its civilization.

Epilogue

The Search Goes On

The pyramids at Giza prompted Ahmed Fakhry to write in his book *The Pyramids:*

> I find that there is no limit to their inspiring beauty. On very dark nights those huge, black, triangular shapes loom up against the sky to connect heaven and earth. People are gay and noisy when they visit the pyramids by day, but at night the romantic beauty of the site and the realization of its antiquity turn the frivolous visitor into a quiet and serious admirer.

The first-century A. D. Roman writer Pliny condemned the pyramids as an "idle and foolish exhibition of wealth." Perhaps the same could be said about any monument built on a grand scale. Yet visitors to these monuments, particularly the pyramids, are glad that they are there—silent witnesses to ancient civilizations with the skill and knowledge to dazzle people thousands of years later. As long as the pyramids have the power to evoke reactions such as Fakhry's, they can truly be said to have magical powers.

And their mysteries continue to tantalize scientists, architects, historians, and others. Why were they built? Were they built for some purpose other

than "idle and foolish" exhibitions of wealth? How were they built? Could there be any truth in the belief that they are somehow cursed? What is exciting is that not all the answers have yet been sifted out of the desert sand. Many of the pyramids have not been excavated; neither have all the tombs and monuments that surround the pyramids. Perhaps answers lie in the shimmering Egyptian desert—on a scrap of ancient papyrus, on an inscription on the wall of a tomb, in the form of a tool or other artifact that will open new veins of speculation and conjecture. Perhaps the answers wait—brooding, silent, expectant, like the pyramids themselves—for a visitor from another time, another place, to put age-old questions to rest.

The silent ruins of the Giza pyramids. What undiscovered secrets do they hold?

For Further Exploration

John Baines and Jaromír Málek, *Atlas of Ancient Egypt.* New York: Facts on File, 1980.

Lionel Casson, *Ancient Egypt. The Great Ages of Man.* Alexandria, VA: Time-Life Books, 1978.

A. Rosalie David, *The Egyptian Kingdoms.* Oakland, CA: Equinox, 1988.

George Hart, *Eyewitness Book: Ancient Egypt.* New York: Knopf, 1990.

David MacCauley, *Pyramid.* Boston: Houghton Mifflin, 1975.

Lila Perl, *Mummies, Tombs, and Treasure: Secrets of Ancient Egypt.* New York: Clarion Books, 1987.

Miriam Stead, *Egyptian Life.* Cambridge, MA: Harvard University Press, 1986.

Philipp Vandenberg, *The Curse of the Pharaohs.* Translated by Thomas Weyr. Philadelphia: Lippincott, 1975.

Works Consulted

Cyril Aldred, *Egypt to the End of the Old Kingdom.* London: Thames and Hudson, 1965.

Leonard Cottrell, *Mountains of Pharaohs.* London: Hale, 1956.

I.E.S. Edwards, *The Pyramids of Egypt.* Middlesex, England: Penguin, 1949.

Ahmed Fakhry, *The Pyramids.* Chicago: University of Chicago Press, 1969.

T.G.H. James, *Excavating in Egypt.* Chicago: University of Chicago Press, 1982.

William Kingsland, *The Great Pyramid in Fact and in Theory,* 2 volumes. London: Rider, 1932.

Kurt Mendelssohn, *The Riddle of the Pyramids.* New York: Praeger, 1974.

Richard Proctor, *The Great Pyramid: Observatory, Tomb, and Temple.* London: Chatto and Windus, 1883.

John Romer, *Ancient Lives: Daily Life in Egypt of the Pharaohs.* New York: Holt, Rinehart, Winston, 1984.

Zecharia Sitchin, "The Great Pyramid Forgery," *Fate,* July 1993.

Peter Tompkins, *Secrets of the Great Pyramid.* New York: Harper and Row, 1971.

John Anthony West, *Ancient Egypt.* NY: Knopf, 1985.

Index

About the Author

Michael O'Neal was born in Elyria, Ohio, in 1949. While he was an undergraduate English major at Bowling Green State University, he developed a strong interest in books and writing. He served in the armed forces and then returned to Bowling Green to earn his doctorate. A former college teacher, O'Neal is a professional writer and editor. He lives in Evergreen, Colorado, with his wife. This is his fifth book in the Great Mysteries series.

Picture Credits